COUNTRIES OF THE WORLD

RUSSIA

RUTH JENKINS

Evans

TITLES IN THE COUNTRIES OF THE WORLD SERIES:

ARGENTINA • AUSTRALIA • BRAZIL • CANADA • CHILE CHINA • EGYPT • FRANCE • GERMANY • INDIA • INDONESIA ITALY • JAPAN • KENYA • MEXICO • NIGERIA • POLAND RUSSIA • SOUTH KOREA • SPAIN • SWEDEN • UNITED KINGDOM USA • VIETNAM

Published by Evans Brothers Limited
2A Portman Mansions
Chiltern Street
London W1U 6NR

VISIT OUR WEBSITE
www.evansbooks.co.uk

First published 2006
© copyright Evans Brothers 2006

British Library Cataloguing in Publication Data
Jenkins, Ruth
Russia. – (Countries of the world)
1.Russia (Federation) – Juvenile literature
I.Title
947'086

ISBN 0 237 52854 1
13-digit ISBN (from 1 January 2007) 978 0 237 52854 6

Editor: Clare Weaver
Designer: Mayer Media Ltd
Picture research: Lynda Lines and Frances Bailey
Map artwork by Peter Bull
Charts and graph artwork by
Encompass Graphics Ltd

Produced for Evans Brothers Limited by
Monkey Puzzle Media Limited
Gissing's Farm, Fressingfield
Suffolk IP21 5SH, UK

Picture acknowledgements
Corbis 16 (Gregor M Schmid); Empics 49 (Sergey Chirikov/EPA); Getty Images front cover lower middle (Macduff Everton/The Image Bank), 9 (Ian Walton), 11 (Hulton Archive), 14 (Chris Niedenthal/Time & Life Pictures), 15 (AFP), 23 top (Ben Radford), 23 bottom (Scott Peterson), 32 (Alexander Nemenov/AFP), 39 (Oleg Nikishin), 43 (Alexander Nemenov/AFP), 45 (Denis Sinyakov/AFP), 46 (Denis Sinyakov/AFP), 53 (Vladimir Suvorov/AFP), 55, back endpaper (Demetrio Carrasco/Stone); Mark Henley 24, 41 top; Eye Ubiquitous/ Hutchison 33 (A Grachtchencov), 38 (Victoria Ivleva-Yorke), 50 bottom (Mrs Bobby Meyer); Novosti UK 12 (G Petrusev), 22, 52 (Vladimir Vyatkin), 54 (RIA Photo News); Panos Pictures 36 (Gerd Ludwig/ Visum); Photolibrary.com front cover top (Jon Arnold), 57 (Martyn Colbeck); Reuters 31 (Alexander Natruskin), 42, 47, 48; Robert Harding World Imagery 44 (Sylvain Grandadam); Sovfoto/Eastfoto 37 (Vanya Edwards/Photographers Direct); Still Pictures front cover upper middle (Tass/Sovfoto), front cover bottom (Tass/Sovfoto), front endpaper (Tass/Sovfoto), 6–7 (Tass/Sovfoto), 13 (Sovfoto/Eastfoto), 18 top (Tass/Sovfoto), 21 (Novosti/ Sovfoto), 25 (Tass/Sovfoto), 26 (Tass/Sovfoto), 28 (Tass/Sovfoto), 30 (Tass/Sovfoto), 34 (Tass/Sovfoto), 35 (Tass/Sovfoto), 41 bottom (Tass/Sovfoto), 50 top (Tass/ Sovfoto); Topfoto.co.uk 5 (Novosti), 8 (Novosti), 10 (Novosti), 18 bottom (Novosti), 19 (Novosti), 20 (Novosti), 29 (Novosti), 40 (Novosti), 51 (National Pictures), 61 (Novosti).

Endpapers (front): Tower blocks dominate the landscape in a newly built residential district of the Russian capital, Moscow.

Title page: A scene in an indoor food market in Moscow.

Imprint and Contents pages: The Volga River flowing through Nizhny Novgorod, one of Russia's most important industrial cities.

Endpapers (back): A winter scene at Dambai, in the Caucasus mountains.

The flag of the
Russian Federation.

At 5,643m, Mount Elbrus (meaning 'snowy mountain') is the highest summit in Europe.

Russia is a huge country. It is so enormous that train journeys are measured in days, not hours. Those living in the east are hard at work while those in the west are sleeping soundly in their beds. While people in the north are battling with sub-zero temperatures and cruel winds in the winter, temperatures in the south are mild enough to ensure the survival of tea plantations along the coast of the Caspian Sea.

The Russian Federation is the largest of the independent states to emerge from the break-up of the Union of Soviet Socialist Republics (USSR) in 1991. Russia is the world's largest country, almost twice the size of the USA, straddling the continents of Europe and Asia and 11 time zones. Within this great expanse, you will find the craggy slopes of Europe's highest mountain, Mount Elbrus, and the Volga, Europe's longest river. Nestled at the heart of Siberia is Lake Baikal, the world's deepest lake.

Once you have taken in Russia's staggering size, the next challenges are to understand its stormy history, and the diversity of its culture, past and present.

Centuries of rule by tsars (meaning emperors, and sometimes written as czar or tzar) were brought to an abrupt end in the early twentieth century. Over 1.7 million Russian soldiers died while fighting Germany in the First World War. This brutal waste triggered rioting across the Russian Empire, leading to a revolution in 1917. The last tsar, Nicholas II, abdicated (gave up his throne) and was exiled to Siberia, where he and his family were eventually executed. Lenin became leader, and the world's first Marxist (Communist) government was set up.

The USSR was born in 1922, and after the Second World War (1939–45) it emerged as a world superpower. The USSR and the USA were enemies during a period known as the Cold War, which lasted from the late 1940s to the late 1980s. The USSR pioneered space exploration with the launch of the first space satellite *Sputnik 1* in 1957, and its athletes were among the best in the world. Yet the realities of everyday life in the USSR were poorly understood by those outside its borders, because the communist regime allowed few outsiders to visit, and fewer of its citizens to travel abroad.

The USSR broke up in December 1991, and Russia's borders opened up to visitors. The last decade has seen great changes to Russia's economy, society and the government. Freedom of speech has returned, triggering a

Built by order of Ivan the Terrible, the domes of St Basil's Cathedral dominate Moscow's Red Square.

lively media. There has been a revival of open religious and artistic expression, with many young people in Moscow and St Petersburg experimenting with new forms of art and music.

However, there is a darker side to the new Russia. Environmental pollution was common across the former USSR, and today the country is struggling to deal with the effects of this. The health of Russians is affected by pollution, alcoholism and violent crime. Organised crime is rife across many levels of society. International disputes over territory continue, and incidents in Chechnya, which is fighting for independence from Russia, still make news across the world.

RUSSIA'S MAIN CITIES AND NEIGHBOURING COUNTRIES

ARCTIC OCEAN

Chukchi Sea

Zemlya Frantsa Iosifa

Novosibirskiye Ostrova

Severnaya Zemlya

Anadyr

N

NORWAY

SWEDEN

FINLAND

Barents Sea

Murmansk

Novaya Zemlya

Kara Sea

Kola Peninsula

Laptev Sea

Bering Sea

Kamchatka Peninsula

LITHUANIA

RUSSIA

LATVIA

ESTONIA

St Petersburg

Arkhangelsk

Magadan

POLAND

BELARUS

Moscow

Kirov

R U S S I A

Yakutsk

Petropavlovsk-Kamchatsky

Sea of Okhotsk

Kuril Islands

UKRAINE

Nizhny Novgorod

MOLDOVA

Voronezh

Kazan

Perm

Yekaterinburg

Rostov-na-Donu

Samara

Ufa

Omsk

Krasnoyarsk

Khabarovsk

Black Sea

Sochi

Volgograd

Astrakhan

Novosibirsk

Irkutsk

Lake Baikal

TURKEY

GEORGIA

ARMENIA

AZERBAIJAN

Caspian Sea

KAZAKHSTAN

MONGOLIA

CHINA

Vladivostok

Sea of Japan

UZBEKISTAN

0   1500 km

0   1000 miles

NORTH KOREA

JAPAN

TURKMENISTAN

KYRGYZSTAN

SOUTH KOREA

TAJIKISTAN

Peasant farmers have worked under slave-like conditions throughout Russia's history.

Before 1917, the Russian Empire was an autocracy – a state governed by just one ruler – the tsar. Agriculture formed the basis of the economy. Serfs – peasants who were not allowed to leave the land they worked on – provided the main workforce in rural areas.

PRE-REVOLUTIONARY RUSSIA

The reign of the last tsar, Nicholas II, was a troubled one. War with Japan in 1904 was deeply unpopular. Defeats and a lack of civil rights at home sparked protests across the country. On Sunday, 22 January 1905, a priest named Gapon led a group of unhappy, but loyal workers to the palace to protest. As they approached, the palace guards panicked, opening fire on the crowd at point-blank range. The events of 'Bloody Sunday' were condemned around the world.

Strikes, mutinies and assassinations followed, until Nicholas reluctantly agreed to the protestors' demands. In October 1905, he signed a document that promised freedom of speech and an elected parliament – the *Duma*.

In August 1914, Russia declared war on Austria and Germany. The Russian army was extremely short of supplies – one million men did not have rifles, and within two months the army suffered two major defeats. The tsar decided to leave for the war front, leaving his wife Alexandra in charge. Alexandra was unpopular, because of her influence over her husband and her relationship with Rasputin, a notorious monk, whose power angered many (he was murdered by a group of noblemen in 1916). By 1917, the situation had worsened. Troops were deserting, and food prices quadrupled. Discontent had spread like wildfire.

THE REVOLUTION

In February 1917, people queuing for bread began to riot. Instead of calming the crowd, soldiers sent to control them joined in. Law and order disintegrated and people demanded the tsar's abdication. In March, Nicholas gave in, signing an agreement in which he renounced his throne. After the events of

ARCTIC OCEAN

N

St Petersburg

Moscow

Yekaterinburg

Black Sea

Volgograd

Caspian Sea

Irkutsk

Lake Baikal

Petropavlovsk-Kamchatsky

Vladivostok

0   1500 km
0   1000 miles

● Territory lost after 1917

○ Extent of Russian Empire, 1922

— Present boundary of Russian Federation

Bloody Sunday, no European country would accept the exiled tsar. He was sent away to the town of Yekaterinburg in Siberia with his family, where they were executed 18 months later.

A provisional government stepped in. However, with a promise to end the war, a group called the Bolsheviks (led by Vladimir Lenin) seized control during the Great October Socialist Revolution.

Nicholas II and Alexandra, the last tsar and tsarina of Russia.

THE CIVIL WAR

The Bolsheviks renamed themselves the Communist Party, and introduced a series of political reforms. A secret police force called the *Cheka* (later the GPU), and the Red Army were set up. Arrest, torture and execution saw that those who did not believe in communism were eliminated. Full-scale civil war broke out in 1918, during which nine million people died from fighting, famine and disease. A group known as 'The Whites' opposed the Bolsheviks, but with the strength of the Red Army and the *Cheka* behind them, the Bolsheviks retained power.

Civil war ended in 1921, but the country was in tatters. Lenin introduced a controversial New Economic Policy (NEP), which improved agricultural and industrial production. In 1922, the Union of Soviet Socialist Republics (USSR), an alliance of Russia with neighbouring states was established. Lenin died in 1924 and, after a power struggle, Josef Stalin became leader.

RUSSIAN LEADERS SINCE NICHOLAS II

Nicholas II 1894–1917
Alexander Kerensky 1917
Vladimir Lenin 1917–24
Josef Stalin 1929–53
Georgi Malenkov 1953–55
Nikolai Bulganin 1955–58
Nikita Khrushchev 1958–64
Leonid Brezhnev 1964–82
Yuri Andropov 1982–84
Konstantin Chernenko 1984–85
Mikhail Gorbachev 1985–91
Boris Yeltsin 1991–99
Vladimir Putin 2000–

THE STALIN REGIME

Under Stalin's regime, 20–30 million citizens were murdered – the equivalent of half the UK's current population.

ECONOMIC REFORM

Stalin abandoned Lenin's NEP programme and, in 1928, he launched a series of Five-Year Plans to boost production across industries such as mining. They were successful – in the first ten years, Russia's industrial capacity grew rapidly. For example, coal production more than trebled its output between 1928 and 1937.

To increase the amount of food available, Stalin ordered the collectivisation of agriculture. Farmers were ordered to hand over their land, machinery and livestock to collective farms, which were managed by large groups of families.

TERROR

Most farmers resisted Stalin's orders, killing their animals instead of handing them over. Stalin's response was brutal. Grain was confiscated, leading to the death of six million from famine in 1932–33. Millions were exiled to Siberian gulags (death camps).

Farmers were not the only people transported to gulags. Individuals who did not support Stalin were also sent. They were collected from their homes at night by the secret police, and tortured to provide false confessions of wrongdoing.

THE GREAT PATRIOTIC WAR

In 1939, Europe was on the brink of war. The USSR would not sign an alliance with France and the UK. Instead, Stalin stunned the world by signing a deal with Germany. Nevertheless, Hitler invaded the USSR in 1941. Stalin mobilised the USSR in the cause of the 'Great Patriotic War', in which 27 million citizens of the USSR died, but the USSR did not surrender.

The Red Army's success meant that President Roosevelt of the USA and British Prime Minister Churchill had to agree to Stalin's post-war plans. Consequently, the USSR was allowed to govern the areas it liberated (most of Eastern Europe) until elections were held. Soviet foreign policy supported communist groups who later secured power.

After the war, using resources taken from

Harvesting grain on a collective farm in 1933.

In September 1941, during the Second World War, the German army surrounded Leningrad. The siege lasted 872 days. Nearly one million people died from bombing, starvation and disease. As the Germans approached the city, many people escaped – but nearly three million were trapped.

There was no heating or water supply, and very little food. In desperation, people ate their pets, rats and birds. In January and February 1942 alone, 200,000 people died,

With water supplies cut off, women resort to collecting water from broken water mains.

but Leningrad's citizens bravely struggled on. The siege was finally lifted on 27 January 1944.

Germany, Stalin modernised industry, and nuclear weapons were developed. The USSR emerged as a world superpower, ready to challenge capitalist USA. Hostility between the two powers deepened, and the Cold War began. The North Atlantic Treaty Organisation (NATO) was set up in 1949 to protect Western Europe against invasion from the USSR.

AFTER STALIN

Stalin died in 1953, leaving a power struggle in the Communist Party. Following the short-lived premierships of Malenkov and Bulganin, Nikita Khrushchev became leader. Khrushchev denounced Stalin's murderous regime, but he brought the world to the brink of nuclear war during the 1962 Cuban Missile Crisis. The USSR allegedly placed nuclear missiles on the island of Cuba, within striking distance of the USA. Khrushchev claimed that they were put there to protect Cuba from invasion by the USA. Others suspect that the USSR was retaliating against nuclear missiles installed by the USA in Turkey, Italy and West Germany, from where they could be launched against the USSR. Fortunately, diplomatic negotiations resolved the dispute, and the USSR backed off.

Khrushchev lost power two years later to Leonid Brezhnev, who drained the USSR's economy to finance the Cold War. Consumer goods became scarce, industry crumbled and human rights were again curtailed. Brezhnev died in 1982.

THE USSR, 1922–1991

THE DEMISE OF THE USSR

In 1985, Mikhail Gorbachev became general secretary of the Communist Party and a new era of change began.

ECONOMIC REFORM

Gorbachev's two main policies were *Glasnost* (openness) and *Perestroika* (restructuring). These important policies forced the USSR to face its economic, environmental and social problems.

A new parliament was formed in 1988. Most of its members were voted for directly by the people, creating a sense of political freedom.

THE END OF THE USSR

The influence of the USSR across Eastern Europe declined, reaching a spectacular finale in November 1989 when the Berlin Wall, a symbol of division between Eastern and Western Europe, was pulled down. Not only were East and West Germany reunited, but the Cold War was effectively over.

Jubilant crowds gather on the western side of the Berlin Wall, as the GDR (East Germany) opens its borders in 1989.

Change also spread across the USSR. Republics such as Lithuania campaigned for independence and, in June 1991, Boris Yeltsin became president of the Russian Republic.

In December, Yeltsin met with leaders of Belarus and Ukraine to discuss the future. They declared that the USSR no longer existed, and proclaimed a new Commonwealth of Independent States (CIS), an alliance between all the newly independent states. Gorbachev was now a president without a country, and he resigned on 25 December. Boris Yeltsin was in charge of the largest and most powerful state – the Russian Federation.

FROM YELTSIN TO PUTIN

Yeltsin began the process of introducing a more open economy in Russia. This involved privatising state businesses, housing, land and agriculture, and allowing the market rather

GNI PER CAPITA (US$)

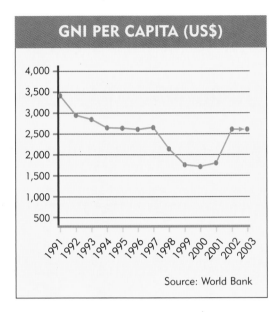

4,000
3,500
3,000
2,500
2,000
1,500
1,000
500

1991 1992 1993 1994 1995 1996 1997 1998 1999 2000 2001 2002 2003

Source: World Bank

than the state to determine prices. Many of the former state industries were handed over to a small number of individuals, who became a new breed of super rich businessmen – the 'oligarchs'. The new economy brought problems: homelessness, inflation, organised crime and corruption.

INTERNATIONAL DISPUTES

Aggressive fighting with Chechnya in the 1990s, a predominantly Islamic republic in the Caucasus region, attracted criticism. Chechen territory has a strategic importance to Russia, as oil pipelines from the Caspian Sea have to travel through Chechnya on their way to Russia. Chechnya is perceived as a threat for several reasons. It is thought to supply a number of the violent gangs operating in Russia, and to have been responsible for bombing campaigns in Moscow. By 1997, at least 25,000 people had died in the fighting.

Yeltsin's power began to decline. The media often portrayed him as a man who was drunk, paranoid and helpless. In a surprise move, he resigned in late 1999, and Prime Minister Vladimir Putin became president in 2000.

Putin retains majority support in Russia today. The economy has shown signs of recovery, thanks to healthy oil and gas exports. He has cracked down on crime and violence, though with limited success. Putin has also taken an uncompromising stance on terrorism, continuing the war in Chechnya.

CASE STUDY
CHECHEN REBELS STORM MOSCOW THEATRE

On 23 October 2002, 40 Chechen rebels, strapped with explosives, stormed a Moscow theatre during a performance. Over 800 people were taken hostage, as the rebels demanded an end to the war with Chechnya.

Negotiations lasted three days, before Russian Special Forces raided the building, pumping in a poisonous gas. All the rebels were killed, but 129 hostages also died, causing public outcry.

Russian TV shows Chechen hostage-takers strapped with explosives inside the theatre.

Elk roam the coniferous forest near Kostroma. Attempts at domesticating the elk have largely failed.

C limate across the whole of Russia is continental, with extreme ranges of temperature. The winters are long, dark, and very cold, but the summers can be stiflingly hot. The landscape is remarkably flat, interrupted only by the Ural Mountains, which form a low snaking line no more than 1,900m high, from the Barents Sea in the north, to the Caspian Sea in the south. The Urals are a natural barrier dividing European and Asian Russia.

CLIMATE AND VEGETATION

A set of climate and vegetation bands stretch across Russia from west to east. The most northerly belt, found in areas within the Arctic Circle, is called tundra. Here, the ground is permanently frozen, insulated by a blanket of snow in winter. Warmer temperatures in the short summers allow a bed of moss and lichen to erupt, interspersed with lakes and pools of water.

The next band is taiga. It is an area of forest, where pine, larch, spruce and fir trees grow. It is a rich home to wildlife – deer, wolves, foxes and elk, a type of large deer.

Taiga gives way to mixed leaf forest, where most of the trees are deciduous (they lose their leaves in the autumn). The main type of tree is birch. As you move further south, steppe becomes the dominant vegetation. The steppe is a type of grassland, with very few trees and rich, dark soil called *chernozyom*, or black earth. Traditionally, the steppe has been used for grazing and cultivation, but overgrazing has led to soil erosion in some places, and desertification (transformation of the land into desert) is a threat.

NORTH EUROPEAN RUSSIA

European Russia is larger than any other European country, but accounts for just a quarter of Russia's total area. The region includes arctic conditions: the Zemlya Frantsa Iosifa island group is so far north that it reaches the area of the Arctic Sea that is permanently frozen. However, across most of the region, summers are cool and short, and winters are snowy. The main vegetation types in this region are taiga and broadleaf forest. Moscow and St Petersburg lie within the 500km-wide band of broadleaf forest.

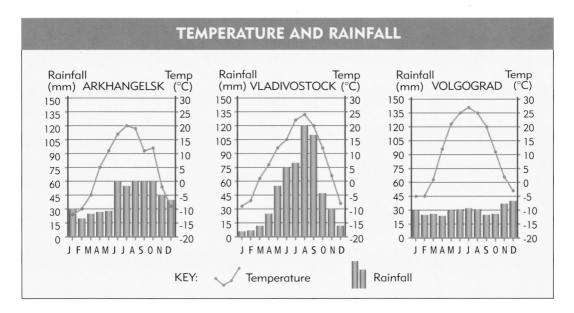

TEMPERATURE AND RAINFALL

ARKHANGELSK
Rainfall (mm) / Temp (°C)

VLADIVOSTOCK
Rainfall (mm) / Temp (°C)

VOLGOGRAD
Rainfall (mm) / Temp (°C)

J F M A M J J A S O N D

KEY: Temperature — Rainfall

KARELIA

To the north-east of St Petersburg lies the Republic of Karelia (sometimes spelt Kareliya), a richly forested area on the border with Finland. Here are the oldest and most biologically diverse forests in Europe, protected by Russian and international law. However, in the early 1990s, many international companies came into the area to harvest timber. Vast areas of forest were destroyed, but little attempt has been made to plant new trees to compensate for those cut down.

Karelia has over 60,000 lakes, including Europe's largest two: Lake Ladoga and Lake Onega. In winter, brave swimmers take a dip in the lakes. A hole is cut into the ice to provide easy access.

THE VOLGA

The source of the Volga river, the main part of European Russia's river network, is found in the Valdai Hills in the European North. The Volga flows south for 3,530km before emptying into the Caspian Sea at Astrakhan.

RUSSIA'S REGIONS (EUROPEAN RUSSIA, SIBERIA AND THE FAR EAST)

SOUTH EUROPEAN RUSSIA

South European Russia is warmer and more mountainous than the north. The Caucasus mountain range – stretching between the Black and Caspian Seas, is home to Mount Elbrus, Europe's highest mountain. It rarely freezes along the Black Sea coast, and conditions are mild enough to grow tea, citrus fruit and grapes for wine-making.

CLIMATE AND VEGETATION

South of the cities of Saratov and Voronezh, mixed leaf forest gives way to a band of steppe vegetation. This is excellent for growing crops, particularly wheat. The steppe is also used for grazing sheep, but overgrazing has lead to desertification around the Caspian Sea.

MOUNTAINS

At 5,643m, nestled in the centre of the Caucasus Mountains is Mount Elbrus – a gently sloping volcano and Europe's highest mountain. Glaciers smother the whole of Elbrus and another volcano, Mount Kazbak. Despite the beautiful scenery, tourism is relatively undeveloped in the Caucasus, although there are some ski resorts where heli-skiing is taking off.

THE BLACK SEA

The Black Sea is an inland sea, fed by several rivers including the River Don. The sea can only support life within the top 200m, as underneath

Sunbathers on the beach at Sochi, a popular spa town on the Black Sea coast.

it is contaminated by hydrogen sulphide. Nevertheless, it is home to three species of dolphin, many types of fish and jellyfish.

SOCHI

Some Russian families spend their summer holidays at Sochi, a pebble beach resort on the Black Sea coast. The Caucasus Mountains shelter the town from poor weather, and so the climate is like that of the Mediterranean. Temperatures range from 20 to 27°C from mid-May to September. Former presidents of the USSR, including Stalin, Khrushchev and Brezhnev, had country houses (*dachas*) close to the town.

Although temperatures near the Black Sea coast can be mild, parts of South European Russia can still be extremely cold in the winter – harsh enough for the River Volga to freeze.

VOLGA DELTA

A delta has formed where the Volga empties into the Caspian Sea (the world's largest body of inland water). A delta is a landform that is created when a river meets a large lake or sea and deposits the fine material that it has been carrying, creating a shallow area with sandbanks and mudflats. Deltas are excellent environments for wildlife. In the summer months, the Volga Delta is transformed into a pink and white carpet, as lotus flowers explode into growth. Over 200 types of bird visit the delta, and the surrounding land supports 30 different species of mammal.

The scenery of the 1,000km-long chain of the Caucasus attracts walkers from many countries.

In 1942–43, Stalingrad (now Volgograd) became locked in a ferocious battle that lasted 200 days.

Weather conditions affected the battle's outcome. Summer brought stifling heat, shortages of water and swarms of flies. In the autumn, heavy rains slowed the advance of the German army, as roads disintegrated. When timber used for resurfacing ran out, human bodies were used instead.

The bitter winter brought further hardship, as minus temperatures froze everything solid – from the ground, to aircraft engines.

Suitable clothing was vital. The Red Army had clothing better suited to the conditions than the Germans, but supply problems meant that not all soldiers had access to this essential equipment. The

German soldiers surrender to the Red Army in 1943 in a frozen, war-torn Stalingrad.

Russian Red Army suffered 1.1 million casualties, and 300,000 Germans died.

VEGETATION

- Tundra
- Mountain tundra
- Mountain
- Mixed forest
- Taiga
- Forest steppe
- Steppe
- Semi desert/desert
- Far Eastern forest

N

NORWAY
SWEDEN
FINLAND
Barents Sea
LITHUANIA
RUSSIA   ESTONIA
POLAND   LATVIA
BELARUS
UKRAINE
MOLDOVA
Black Sea
TURKEY   GEORGIA
ARMENIA
AZERBAIJAN
Caspian Sea
KAZAKHSTAN
R U S S I A
Lake Baikal
CHINA
MONGOLIA
UZBEKISTAN
TURKMENISTAN
KYRGYZSTAN
TAJIKISTAN
NORTH KOREA
SOUTH KOREA
JAPAN

0   1500 km
0   1000 miles

SIBERIA AND THE FAR EAST

Siberia and the Russian Far East cover a massive 14 million km² area. The dividing line between Siberia and the Russian Far East is found along the borders of the Chita and Amur regions in the south and the Sakha Republic in the north. The scenery is diverse, from monsoon forest and bubbling geysers, to giant rivers and swarms of lakes.

SIBERIA – CLIMATE AND VEGETATION

Many people picture Siberia as a frozen and remote wilderness, but this is only accurate for part of the year. Siberia's climate is continental, and while temperatures plunge as low as –35°C in winter, they can reach a hot +35°C in the summer.

With the exception of the Altai Mountains in southern Siberia, the landscape is flat. Different bands of vegetation – tundra, taiga and steppe – punctuate the vast space as you travel from north to south.

LAKES AND RIVERS

Siberia is awash with water. It has over 23,000 rivers and more than a million lakes. The major rivers are the Ob, Yenisei and gold-rich Lena, which all flow from south to north. The

Providing meat, milk and transport, domesticated reindeer on the Taimyr Peninsula.

River Amur forms a natural boundary between Russia and China. Lake Baikal, the world's deepest lake, is home to a vast collection of unique wildlife like the nerpa seal, and is perhaps Siberia's most spectacular natural feature.

THE FAR EAST – CLIMATE AND VEGETATION

Climate in the Far East is similar to that of Siberia. However, one particular region has a very different climate. Ussuriland, in the south-east, has a northern monsoon climate. This means that it has more rain and slightly milder winters – temperatures usually fall no lower than –13°C in January.

VOLCANOES

The 1,200km-long Kamchatka Peninsula holds Russia's most dramatic mountain range. There are about 200 volcanoes, 68 of which still erupt, including the 4,750m high Klyuchevskaya, the region's highest peak. The volcanic chain continues beyond the peninsula to the Kuril Islands, part of the Pacific 'Ring of Fire,' a zone notorious for its frequent earthquake and volcano activity.

GEYSERS

Geysers, springs that throw up jets of hot, steamy water, are found in great abundance within the 'Valley of Geysers' in the Kronotsky national park (south-eastern Kamchatka). With over 200 individual geysers, the Geyser River bubbles constantly. They heat the river to an abnormal 27°C (warmer than most bath water!), making it an impossible environment for fish to survive, but conditions are perfect for colourful algae to grow. It is the second largest geyser field in the world after the well-known Yellowstone Park in the USA.

MONSOON FOREST

Monsoon forest is a unique habitat found only in Ussuriland in the Russian Far East. The relatively warm and wet climate allows lush, dense green forest to grow. The forest shelters many animals, including bears, wolves, the Siberian (or Amur) tiger – the largest member of the cat family, and the Amur leopard. Both of these species are endangered as a result of hunting, but are now protected by law.

Heated water shoots up from the Valley of Geysers in Kamchatka.

Crowds in Nizhny Novgorod, the hub of Russia's manufacturing industry.

R ussia's population is mostly urban, and is concentrated in European Russia's cities. The majority of the population is Russian, but there are over 90 different ethnic groups, with various languages and traditions.

RUSSIA TODAY

POPULATION SIZE AND DISTRIBUTION

In 2004, the Russian population was estimated at 143,782,338. Three-quarters live within European Russia and, of those, almost 75 per cent live in urban areas. Moscow has the largest population with nine million, followed by St Petersburg (four million). Nizhny Novgorod, Samara, Kazan, Perm, Ufa, Rostov-na-Donu and Volgograd are all cities with more than one million inhabitants.

ETHNIC GROUPS

Russia is ethnically diverse. Russians, together with Ukrainians and Belarussians, form an ethnic group known as the Slavs, and account for 85 per cent of Russia's population. Other ethnic groups include the Turkic peoples from the Volga region and the Karelians from near the Finnish border. The Korean and Chinese populations are growing in the Far East,

where there is also a small Inuit community.

In 1989, Russia had a population of one million Jews, but when laws changed to make it easier for them to leave the country, many did so, to escape from prejudice. By 1998, 50 per cent had left Russia, moving to Germany, the USA and Israel. Those who remain are mostly in European Russia.

MIGRATION

The USSR authorities controlled migration (moving from one country to another) tightly, and people required passports to travel within the country. Migration into and away from the USSR was virtually impossible. When the USSR broke up, 25 million ethnic Russians were living outside Russia, in neighbouring states such as Ukraine and Kazakhstan. Three million of these people, who were in areas where economic conditions were deteriorating, decided to return to Russia where living standards were relatively higher. Others, living

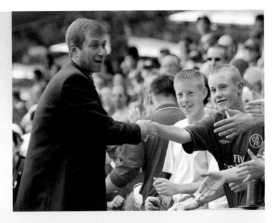

The profile of the 160,000 strong Russian community in London has rocketed in the last few years, propelled by the Russian businessman Roman Abramovich, whose millions have transformed Chelsea Football Club. Today, every 15th property sold for over half a million pounds in London goes to a Russian buyer.

The Russian community is especially visible around the Stratford area of London. There are already two Russian-language weekly newspapers, a magazine

Russian billionaire Roman Abramovich greets Chelsea fans at Stamford Bridge, 2003.

and a radio station, along with Russian restaurants, clubs and grocery shops.

in wealthy areas like Turkmenistan (which is rich in oil and gas resources) have chosen not to return.

Since 1991, 1.1 million people have left Russia – mostly for the USA, Germany and Israel. Many of those migrants include Russia's most educated and highly skilled people. This trend is called a 'brain drain'. Russia's brain drain has led to the loss of engineers, doctors, scientists and teachers.

Another trend to have emerged is human trafficking. Since 1991, up to 500,000 women have left Russia to work as prostitutes,

sometimes against their will. The reasons behind this include high female unemployment, a lack of job opportunities, and a lack of legislation (laws) to deal with the trafficking problem.

Parts of Russia's Far East are showing trends of depopulation (population decline). The three million Chinese who have moved to this region counter this trend. Some Russians have called for border controls with China to be tightened, amid fears that this Chinese group might seek to break the territory away from Russia and put it into Chinese hands.

A Chinese trader at a Chinese market in Isiriisk, in Russia's Far East.

URBAN AND RURAL LIFE

Today, the majority of Russian people live in urban areas. When Khrushchev allowed people to move around the country more freely, people abandoned the countryside in search of a better life. However, many cities grew extremely rapidly, and the government struggled to provide adequate housing and facilities. Today, continued under-investment and industrial decline have had a huge impact on life in urban and rural areas.

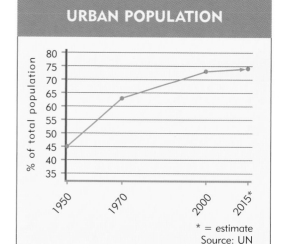

URBAN POPULATION

% of total population

* = estimate
Source: UN

INDUSTRIAL DECLINE

Cities grew rapidly in relatively remote areas of Russia, where rich natural resources fuelled the pre- and post-war industrial boom. Not all industries were efficient, however, and some have struggled to compete globally since the collapse of communism. For the workers caught up in this economic downturn, there have been serious consequences. Some have had to take on multiple jobs or grow their own food. Others have lost both their jobs and their homes.

CITY LIFE

The majority of city inhabitants live in tiny high-rise flats. Conditions are cramped – the average living area for each person in Russia is 16.1m², compared to 60m² in the USA. Larger flats usually house extended families. Five and a half million people live in communal flats

Young mothers outside typical housing blocks on the outskirts of Moscow.

(*komunalki*), which have just one room shared by the whole family. Kitchens and bathrooms are shared with other families. Richer Russians are starting to buy up these flats. They knock several *komunalki* together to create larger apartments.

Moscow is one of the most expensive cities in the world. The cost of food and clothing is comparable with cities in Western Europe, but salaries are significantly lower. Teachers, for example, receive wages that are about one thirtieth of an average London teacher's salary.

RURAL LIFE

Stalin introduced an unpopular policy of collectivisation, where small farms were forcibly amalgamated. This allowed the government to control the distribution of food across the country, but workers on the farms were treated almost like slaves. They were not allowed to leave, they were prevented from showing initiative or implementing their own ideas, and they received low wages.

Rural villagers gather twigs to make brooms, which are sold to subsidise meagre pensions.

After Stalin's death, the restrictions on movement were lifted, and the government tried to improve rural conditions. Yet many people did not think that enough was done – poverty was still a big problem, so people left for the cities in large numbers.

In the 1990s, when the USSR fell apart, rural Russians were given the option to buy the land they worked on. Those who could afford to do this built up large properties, and became part of a new rural elite. For poorer people, the outlook is less optimistic. Many former collective farm workers have lost the few privileges they had, such as free housing and schooling. Old farm buildings lie crumbling, while poverty and feelings of isolation have increased. The 2002 census in Russia revealed that 35,000 villages in Russia have no more than ten inhabitants.

POPULATION DECLINE

The population of the Russian Federation has been falling since 1991. By 2050, the population is expected to have tumbled to 121,256,000. Life expectancy is also declining. In 2001, average life expectancy was just 66 years, compared to 80 years in nearby Sweden.

THE IMPACT OF WAR AND STALIN

During the Second World War, 27 million citizens of the USSR died – the equivalent of nearly half of the UK's population today. People who might have gone on to have families were killed before they could have children. The disproportionate number of male deaths also meant many women

CASE STUDY
LIFE EXPECTANCY ON
THE KOLA PENINSULA

The Kola Peninsula is in the far north-west of the Russian Federation. It is home to two nickel processing factories owned by the Norilsk Nickel company, Russia's biggest contributor to air pollution. The UN Environmental Commission describes the area around the three cities of Nickel, Zapolyarny and Monchegorsk as a zone of 'ecological catastrophe'.

Nickel ore contains sulphur. When nickel ore is processed, sulphur dioxide is released into the atmosphere, causing acid rain. Acid rain has killed thousands of hectares of forest. Workers and those who live close to the factories face serious

health problems. In 1992, the life expectancy of those living in and around Nickel plummeted to just 34 years.

Air pollution travels across international boundaries very easily, and it has damaged forests in Norway, Sweden and Finland. Since 1970, these countries have placed pressure on Russia to reduce the amount of sulphur dioxide it produces. Fortunately, Russia has managed to meet targets to reduce air pollution set by an important law called the International Convention on Long-Range Transboundary Air Pollution (LRTAP).

Causing chronic air pollution, Severonikel metals plant in Monchegorsk, Murmansk.

were unable to marry or start a family.

Stalin's terror purges and forced famines eliminated a further 20–30 million people during the years before and after the war. All of these factors have had a lasting effect on population growth in Russia.

SMALLER FAMILIES

After the loss of so many men during the Second World War, women were encouraged to work. Housing shortages, a lack of childcare facilities and economic hardship meant that many women chose to have fewer children in the 1950s. By the 1970s, high divorce and abortion rates (after an abortion, some women can become infertile) meant that even fewer women had children.

In the 1980s and 1990s, high levels of unemployment made life stressful for many Russians. Worried about the financial burden, some families chose to have fewer children.

HEALTH

Health also influences population growth and decline. Hospitals receive very little funding from the government, which means they have inadequate resources to treat patients.

Pollution will continue to have an impact on Russia's people for many years. Half of the population have contaminated water supplies;

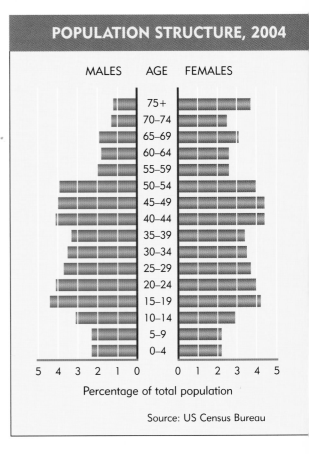

POPULATION STRUCTURE, 2004

MALES   AGE   FEMALES

Percentage of total population

Source: US Census Bureau

others suffer from diseases caused by air pollution. Mortality (death) rates have also risen as a result of increases in violent crime (such as murder) and alcoholism, which can cause fatal diseases like cirrhosis of the liver.

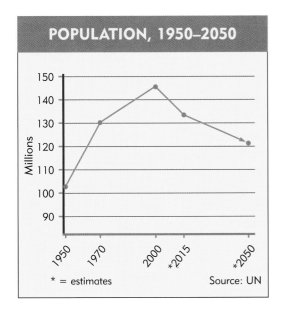

POPULATION, 1950–2050

Millions

1950   1970   2000   *2015   *2050

* = estimates   Source: UN

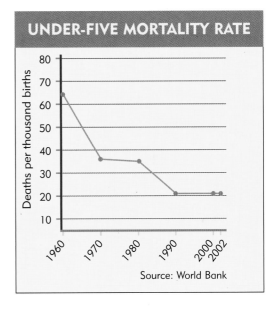

UNDER-FIVE MORTALITY RATE

Deaths per thousand births

1960   1970   1980   1990   2000 2002

Source: World Bank

27

Combine harvesters gather grain on a collective farm in Bashkiria.

Agriculture accounts for just 4.9 per cent of Russia's GDP (Gross Domestic Product), but is more efficient than it was. In the 1980s, Russia had to import large amounts of wheat from the USA. Since 2001, thanks to better management and crop varieties, Russia has switched to being a net exporter of wheat. Major crops include wheat, barley, potatoes and sugar beet. Poultry, beef, pork and dairy products are also produced.

AGRICULTURE

STALIN'S LEGACY

Conditions on the collective farms introduced by Stalin were very hard and there were few facilities for local people. After Stalin's death, many workers left the farms to go and work in the cities instead. Rural areas still suffer from depopulation, and the agricultural workforce is relatively old.

GROW YOUR OWN!

After 1991, townspeople were allowed to rent small areas of land from the state. This land was used to grow fresh fruit and vegetables, which were hard to find in local shops. Some people even have cottages (*dachas*) on these allotments.

These allotments are currently under threat. In 2002, President Putin signed an agreement to allow big companies to buy up large areas of land. This could make it difficult for people to continue this practice.

AGRICULTURAL REGIONS

Most agriculture is concentrated in south-western European Russia, where the climate is favourable. The northern Caucasus region is particularly productive. Many different types of fruit and vegetables – including citrus fruit – grow well there. The hill slopes are also used to cultivate a rare, oily type of tobacco and the landscape is lined with vineyards. The grape harvest is used to create one of Russia's finest champagnes.

DACHAS

The word *dacha* means 'summer escape from the city'. *Dachas* are country cottages, where some Russians spend the weekend relaxing, often growing vegetables in their gardens.

CHINESE FARMERS

The Far East is attracting a new group of farmers: the Chinese. Until now, Russia has imported food from China, but China is now having difficulty growing enough food for its population. There is not enough farmland in China, so some Chinese farmers cross the border each spring to grow vegetables on Russian territory. In 2004, there were 2,390 Chinese farm workers in the Primorye province alone.

This group of farmers make a living by selling their produce at local Russian markets – it is too expensive to take it back to China to sell. This has caused some conflict with Russian farmers, who have accused Chinese farmers of taking over the market. However, as most young Russians choose to leave the region, it is likely that the number of Chinese people working the land will increase further.

GRAIN EXPORTS AND IMPORTS, 1994–2003

Million tonnes (y-axis: 0, 2, 4, 6, 8, 10, 12, 14)
Years (x-axis): 1994, 1995, 1996, 1997, 1998, 1999, 2000, 2001, 2002, 2003

— Imports
— Exports

Source: NAG Consulting

CASE STUDY
KRASNODARSKY TEA

Along with vodka, tea is an important national drink in Russia. Russians traditionally drink their tea heavily sweetened, with sugar, jam or honey.

Along the Black Sea coastline lies the town of Dagomys. The town is home to the most northerly tea plantations in the world. Thanks to the relatively warm climate (the average annual temperature is 18°C), tea plants are able to thrive and tours of the tea plantations are a popular attraction for tourists to the area.

Tea is picked by machine on a plantation.

FORESTRY

Siberia's forests (taiga) cover an area of more than 3 million km^2 and contain one fifth of all the world's trees. Since the collapse of the USSR, the Russian government has invited foreign companies to log the forest, in an effort to boost the economy. The industry employs 20 per cent of the Russian workforce. As a result, Russian forests are disappearing at a rate of 12 million hectares a year. Organisations such as the Siberian Forests Project are campaigning hard to persuade the Russian government to protect the taiga.

LOGGING

The Siberian taiga has been logged since the 1950s. The wood from these trees is a very valuable resource, used in construction and furniture-making across the world. The taiga is endangered by illegal logging, which generates US$300 million a year but destroys the forest. Most illegal logging uses a technique called skimming, where only one or two high quality trees are used for every ten cut down. To counteract this, it is important for companies that import timber to ensure it has been harvested in a responsible way.

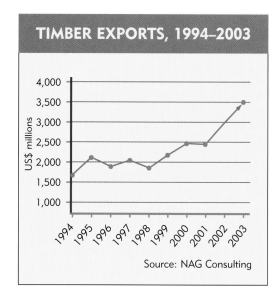

TIMBER EXPORTS, 1994–2003

Source: NAG Consulting

Logging of trees in the Siberian taiga is controversial but it provides valuable income.

According to the WWF (World Wide Fund for Nature), illegal timber is being sold in the UK and other European countries. At the moment, up to 50 per cent of Russian timber is cut down illegally.

Timber suppliers can join the WWF producers group, enabling them to prove to buyers that their forests have been managed properly.

Greenpeace activists outside the Finnish embassy in Moscow, protesting against illegal logging.

Forest and Trade Networks (FTNs) can help buyers do this. FTNs promote careful management of forests, and have certified one million hectares of forest in Russia. In these areas, new trees are planted to replace those that have been harvested, so that the forest will be protected for the future. People who buy timber from these groups know that it has not been cut down illegally.

CONSEQUENCES

If the illegal timber trade continues, the environmental consequences could be devastating. Important wildlife habitats would be lost, making it difficult for rare animal species such as the wolf and bear to survive.

People are also affected. The Siberian forests are home to several indigenous peoples, such as the Khanty or Udege, who depend on the land for hunting, fishing and raising reindeer. When the forests disappear, their way of life is endangered. These people are campaigning to ensure that they have a say in the future of the taiga.

Siberia's rivers are under threat, too. They are used to transport logs to processing plants, but sometimes become blocked, and thousands of hectares of land are flooded.

River ecosystems are also damaged by soil erosion, which occurs when large areas of trees are cut down at once.

Trees perform an important role in the battle against global warming. Carbon dioxide, one of the main gases that cause global warming, is removed from the atmosphere by trees when they grow. Since the taiga is so large, it can remove a significant amount of carbon dioxide from the air, and is known as a 'carbon sink'. If the taiga disappeared, the effects of global warming, including severe storms, would be felt across the world.

GLOBAL WARMING

Global warming refers to the accelerated warming of the Earth's atmosphere. It is thought to result from an accumulation of greenhouse gases (such as carbon dioxide and methane), which are released into the atmosphere by human activity. Factors that contribute to global warming include the burning of fossil fuels and the burning of forests.

FISHING

Fishing is an important industry to Russia. It exports 1.5 million tonnes of fish each year, to countries all over the world and the home market consumes another 1.5 million tonnes. Fish is a popular food in Russia, but it has become an expensive luxury for many poorer families.

BEFORE AND AFTER 1990

The Russian fishing industry has undergone considerable change since 1990, when the state-owned fishing fleet was privatised (sold to private companies).

Before 1990, there was a fleet of 450 fishing vessels based in north-western Russia, around the ports of Murmansk and Arkhangelsk. The fleet was managed by a group called 'Northern Fish', and controlled by the government. A variety of fish including herring, cod, mackerel and sardines were caught and sold at Russian markets.

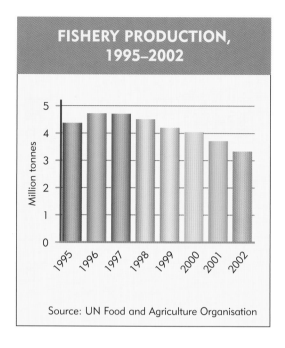

FISHERY PRODUCTION, 1995–2002

Source: UN Food and Agriculture Organisation

A Russian fishing boat in Murmansk, where unemployment has risen since the 1990s.

In the early 1990s, the fishing fleet was divided up among several medium-sized fishing companies, who started to sell the majority of their fish to foreign countries – mostly Norway – but also Denmark, the UK, Spain and Portugal.

These companies decided to concentrate on cod fishing. The main reason for this was that fuel had become very expensive. Catching other species of fish became costly, as boats had to sail further north to catch them. It was also more profitable to sell the fish caught in the Barents and Norwegian Seas to Norwegian ports, where they could charge higher prices, and avoid heavy taxes.

As a result of these changes, unemployment levels have risen among workers whose jobs used to rely on the fishing industry. Fish processing factories, for example, function at a fraction of their original capacity.

There are similar problems in the Russian Far East, where ships and fishing equipment are out of date, and fish processing plants are highly inefficient.

The government has attempted to encourage fishing companies to sell their fish to the Russian market, but this initiative has not been very successful. Incentives cannot match the higher profits obtained by selling to foreign markets.

CASE STUDY
THE DECLINE OF BELUGA STURGEON

The beluga sturgeon is a fish found in the Caspian Sea, and is famed for the high quality caviar (eggs) it produces. Caviar is an edible delicacy around the world, and something of a status symbol.

The beluga sturgeon is the most rare of the three varieties of sturgeon from the Caspian Sea. It can live for 100 years, and grow up to 10m long. The female requires 20 years to mature and begin producing eggs, and it produces the largest grained and most prized of the sturgeon caviars. The beluga is also found in the Black, Azov and Adriatic Seas, as well as the Dnepr and Danube rivers. Demand for beluga caviar is growing around the world as people become wealthier, putting the species under pressure.

The fish has been classified as a threatened species since 1996, owing to illegal poaching (fishing without a licence), over-fishing and pollution of the Caspian Sea. The construction of dams across the rivers leading into the sea means that sturgeon have lost access to all

A woman extracts caviar from a beluga sturgeon. Sturgeon numbers are now falling.

their natural spawning sites (places where they lay their eggs) in rivers. In 1997, the Convention on International Trade in Endangered Species of Wild Fauna and Flora (CITES) passed an agreement to control the sale of sturgeon products, in an attempt to protect the fish. However this legislation has had limited success as adult beluga are thought to no longer breed in the Caspian Sea.

Workers panning river sediment to collect gold at the Angara Company mine.

Russia possesses some of the world's richest natural resources. Underneath Siberia lie large reserves of fossil fuels, including coal, oil and gas. Siberia also has four major goldmines and 800 diamond mines. Russia has inherited serious environmental problems caused by the relentless exploitation of these reserves during the country's period of intensive industrialisation. Renewable energy sources are gradually becoming more important.

ENERGY CONSUMPTION

Russia consumes 7 per cent of the energy used in the world, ranking third behind the USA and China. Russia has the largest natural gas reserves on the planet; so over half of all the energy used is natural gas.

Russia's cold, long winters mean that a lot of energy is needed to heat homes. However, the majority (60 per cent) of all energy is used by Russia's industries.

NUCLEAR POWER

There are currently 10 nuclear power plants with 30 reactors operating in Russia. Despite receiving financial assistance from the USA to improve maintenance, and security to guard against terrorism, the industry is still dated.

The reactors used in Russia are considered by the European Union to be dangerous, and accidents continue to be reported. Regardless of these problems, the country is planning to build 40 new reactors by 2030.

Several areas including Lake Karachay – one of the most polluted spots on Earth – have been contaminated by nuclear waste. In 2001, the government agreed to store and reprocess up to 20,000 tons of foreign high-level nuclear waste. This will earn US$20 billion over the next ten years, but could cause further environmental pollution.

RENEWABLE ENERGY

In addition to its large fossil fuel supplies, Russia also has the resources to produce

CASE STUDY
HYDROELECTRIC POWER IN SIBERIA

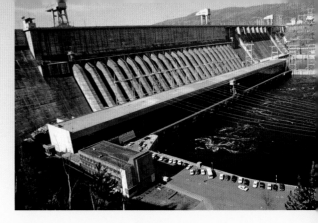

The Krasnoyarsk Dam holds back water from the Angara River to generate HEP.

Hydroelectric power (HEP) is an important component of the Russian energy industry. Between 2005 and 2025, power output from HEP is set to increase by 10 to 15 per cent. Most of this power is generated in Siberia, where the annual volume of water flow is 700km^3, or 20 per cent of the total volume of all Russia's rivers. The total energy capacity of the HEP stations in Siberia is a huge 44.8 billion kilowatt-hours.

Construction of the Krasnoyarsk Dam began in 1961, and was finished 16 years later with the help of 20,000 people. The Krasnoyarsk Dam produces six million kilowatts of electricity each year. The Krasnoyarsk Aluminium Plant, the second largest aluminium plant in the world, uses 70 per cent of this power. The dam is even a popular tourist attraction.

HEP is not without problems, however. The River Yenisei is an important habitat for the Siberian sturgeon, and the dams have affected the fish. In the reservoirs of water behind the dams, the fish grow unusually fast, but they do not mature and do not reproduce well. Pollution from industry also causes problems. These factors have led to the decline of sturgeon populations.

renewable energy. Hydroelectric power provides one fifth of all Russia's energy and this figure will increase. In 2002, the Mutnovskaya geothermal power plant on the Kamchatka Peninsula began service. It was partly financed by a US$100 million grant from the European Bank For Reconstruction and Development.

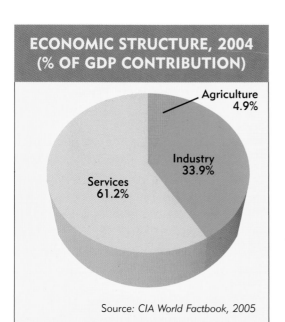

ECONOMIC STRUCTURE, 2004 (% OF GDP CONTRIBUTION)

- Agriculture 4.9%
- Industry 33.9%
- Services 61.2%

Source: CIA World Factbook, 2005

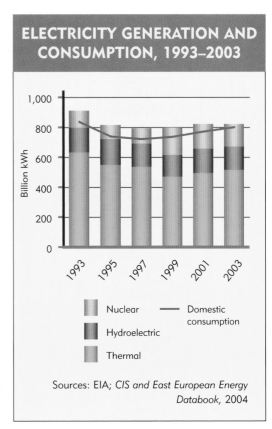

ELECTRICITY GENERATION AND CONSUMPTION, 1993–2003

Billion kWh

Nuclear
Hydroelectric
Thermal
Domestic consumption

Sources: EIA; *CIS and East European Energy Databook*, 2004

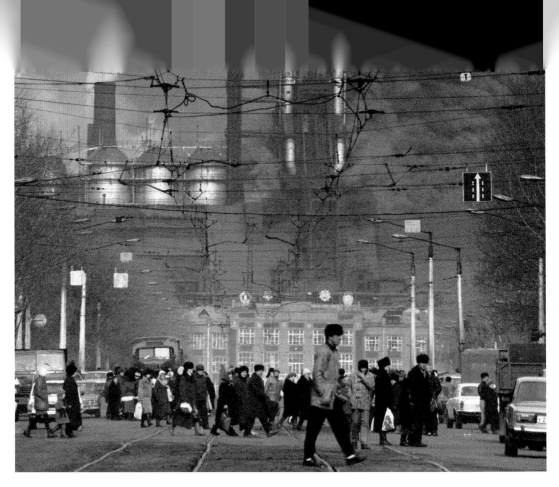

Emissions from the KMK steel plant pollute the air above Novokuznetsk, Siberia.

In 2003, the fifth successive year of economic growth, Russia's economy grew by a healthy 7.3 per cent. Industry is an important part of the economy, accounting for 33.9 per cent of Russian GDP. A quarter of Russia's economic growth is fuelled by energy exports – particularly oil. This dependence on energy means that Russia's economy is vulnerable to fluctuating oil prices and this level of growth may not be guaranteed in the future.

INDUSTRIALISATION

The USSR underwent a rapid period of industrialisation when Stalin was in power. When Germany invaded Russia in 1941, Stalin ordered the evacuation of 1,300 factories and all their employees to the area of relative safety behind the Ural Mountains. The Ural industrial base played an important role in the war, providing 40 per cent of the victorious Red Army's weapons and ammunition.

Industry continued to expand in the region once the war was over. By the late 1980s, the Urals produced one third of all the USSR's steel, and one quarter of all its cast iron. Unfortunately, industry has also brought environmental pollution and health problems to people living in the region.

PRIVATISATION

In the mid-1990s, after the USSR had collapsed, economic reform began. This involved a massive programme of privatisation – industries that had been owned by the state were transferred to private owners. This period

Nestled at the confluence of the Oka and Volga rivers, Nizhny Novgorod is the economic hub of the Volga-Vyatsky region. The city marks the junction of all major transport routes in European Russia, connecting Russia with the Urals. In 2002, the region produced about 2 per cent of Russian GDP. The outlook for the city is positive as it is attracting foreign investment.

The city is home to two of the most famous Soviet engineering firms: MiG, which manufactures aircraft, and GAZ, the Gorky Avto Zavid (Gorky Car Plant), producers of the well-known Volga saloon car. MiG has faced criticism from the humanitarian organisation Amnesty

Military vehicles are built for export in a GAZ-owned factory in Nizhny Novgorod.

International. The company supplies military aircraft to Sudan, which stands accused of providing support to a group of Arab fighters who have allegedly conducted an ethnic cleansing programme, leaving 30,000 people dead and one million homeless.

has been called the 'War of the Oligarchs'. Russia's billionaires fought to control various industries amid rumours of corruption. Competition for the ownership of these industries was fierce, because the new owners would be guaranteed to make a lot of money.

REFORM

Russia's energy sector is still dominated by a few large companies, such as Gazprom, the world's largest gas company. Gazprom produces over 90 per cent of Russian gas and owns over 70 per cent of the country's gas reserves. The Russian government is

attempting to change this situation, so that other companies can come in to compete with Gazprom. This type of reform is important if Russia is to qualify for membership of the World Trade Organisation.

OTHER INDUSTRIES

While the energy sector dominates industry in Russia, the country still has a variety of industries. These include machine building, construction of high-performance aircraft, agricultural machinery and shipbuilding. Medical equipment, scientific instruments, textiles and cars are also manufactured in Russia.

MAJOR TRADING PARTNERS (% OF VALUE), 2003

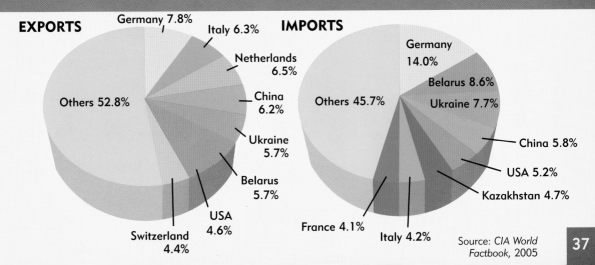

EXPORTS

- Germany 7.8%
- Italy 6.3%
- Netherlands 6.5%
- China 6.2%
- Ukraine 5.7%
- Belarus 5.7%
- USA 4.6%
- Switzerland 4.4%
- Others 52.8%

IMPORTS

- Germany 14.0%
- Belarus 8.6%
- Ukraine 7.7%
- China 5.8%
- USA 5.2%
- Kazakhstan 4.7%
- Italy 4.2%
- France 4.1%
- Others 45.7%

Source: *CIA World Factbook*, 2005

RUSSIA'S ECONOMY – SERVICE INDUSTRIES

Until 1994, services played a very small role in the Russian economy. During the communist period, most services like education and healthcare were either free or extremely cheap, but the quality of those services was often poor.

Today, providing they can afford it, more people are prepared to pay extra money for higher quality services. These industries have grown so much in the last decade, that services now account for 61.2 per cent of Russia's GDP. This growth has attracted foreign investment, particularly from companies based in the USA.

ADVERTISING

Advertising is booming in Russia. There are over 2,000 advertising agencies in Moscow, which devise campaigns to sell all kinds of consumer products and services, from cosmetics to insurance. Advertising campaigns in Russia are similar to those seen in Western Europe and the USA, to the extent that some advertisements are simply dubbed for use on Russian television.

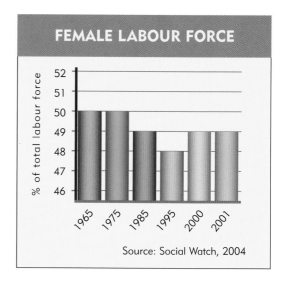

FEMALE LABOUR FORCE

y-axis: % of total labour force

Source: Social Watch, 2004

THE FILM AND MUSIC INDUSTRIES

A large film industry grew up in the days of the USSR. Each town had a cinema, and tickets were cheap. Russia's main film studios are in Moscow and St Petersburg. Since the collapse of communism, and the withdrawal of government subsidies, the Russian film industry has struggled, particularly as it now has to compete with Hollywood. Nevertheless, film-makers have achieved international recognition. For example, the film *Burnt by the Sun*, directed by Nikita Mikhalkov, won an Oscar in 1995.

Live music is popular in Russia, but Russian pop and rock music is not very well known outside the country.

People queue at a Moscow cinema. Since communism's collapse, Hollywood's influence over Russian cinema has grown.

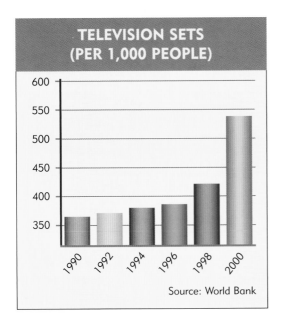

TELEVISION SETS (PER 1,000 PEOPLE)

Source: World Bank

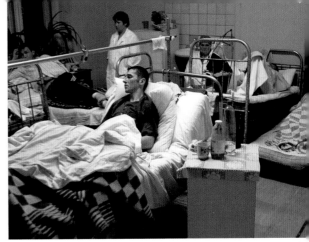

Lack of funds lead to overcrowding in a Kazan hospital. Sometimes, patients have to be left in corridors.

TELECOMMUNICATIONS

The telecommunications industry has the potential to expand rapidly in Russia, as few people have a mobile phone or access to the Internet at home. At the moment, there are just 120 mobile phones and 41 Internet users per 1,000 people, compared to 889 mobile phones and 573 Internet users per 1,000 people in Sweden. The number of foreign Internet Service Providers (ISPs) and mobile phone companies will probably increase to fill this demand.

HEALTHCARE

The healthcare system in Russia is in trouble. There has been little emphasis in the past on prevention of poor health through healthy living. Furthermore, hospitals receive insufficient funding to cope with the growing number of patients suffering from illnesses that range from heart disease, cancer, poisoning and injuries caused by accidents. The lack of money also makes it difficult to maintain hospital buildings and equipment, or continue training medical staff.

The government is working to reform the healthcare system by encouraging private companies to provide healthcare, which people would pay for by taking out medical insurance. This has, in turn, led to a boost to the insurance industry, which provides this medical cover.

TELECOMMUNICATIONS DATA, 2002 (PER 1,000 PEOPLE)

Mainline phones	242
Mobile phones	120
Internet users	41

Source: World Bank

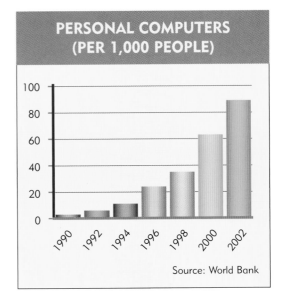

PERSONAL COMPUTERS (PER 1,000 PEOPLE)

Source: World Bank

Some hospitals have special departments where patients go to receive treatment in return for paying a fee. The system is experiencing mixed results, particularly as many Russians are unwilling to pay for medical care, having previously received it for free.

Gridlock in Moscow. The city's planners failed to predict future growth of car ownership.

Russia's transport infrastructure and equipment became quite dilapidated (run down) in the 1980s. Much of the Russian transport network is in need of modernisation and repair.

RAILWAYS

With over 154,000km of track, the railways are Russia's main mode of transport, although they were designed to transport cargo rather than people. The dominance of the railways has arisen for several reasons. Firstly, rail was the most efficient way of transporting goods across Russia's vast territory and, secondly, fuel subsidies favoured the railways over road transport.

As fuel costs have risen, Russian manufacturers are looking for cheaper ways to transport their raw materials and products. For shorter journeys, they will probably look to use trucks and lorries rather than trains. For people, trains are probably the cheapest method of travel, and while journeys may take a long time, the trains are punctual.

ROADS

Roads were not used a great deal during communist times. Few people owned cars and freight was transported by rail, so there was little need to build roads. While roads have been built and maintained in urban areas, roads in rural areas are extremely poor – many areas have not had a new road built since the early twentieth century. The World Bank believes that road transport will become more important in Russia, but a lot of money needs to be spent on repairing and rebuilding roads and bridges across the country.

AIRCRAFT

Aeroflot is the main Russian airline, and it carries the majority of passenger traffic in Russia. In addition, there are over 200 domestic airlines, making it easier to fly between regions without having to travel via Moscow or St Petersburg. Aeroflot now receives fewer state subsidies than in the past, which means that flights have become more expensive, so passenger numbers have declined. The combination of higher fuel and maintenance costs, together with falling passenger numbers, suggest that some of these companies may merge or go out of business in the future.

The Trans-Siberian railway crosses seven time zones during the seven-day, 9,289km journey from Moscow to Vladivostok on the Pacific coast, the longest continuous rail journey in the world.

There are three main railway routes across Siberia: The Rossiya, which never leaves Russia, the Trans-Manchurian, which crosses China, and the Trans-Mongolian, which enters Mongolia.

Construction of the railway began in 1886. Its purposes were to link European Russia with Vladivostok, a major port in the east, to support trade with Asia and to defend Russian territory. Today, the railway is used to transport freight, passengers and tourists.

Crowds gather to board the Trans-Siberian Express. It is a popular tourist magnet.

PUBLIC TRANSPORT

Six Russian cities have underground (metro) systems. The first station was built in Moscow in 1935, but there are also metro systems in St Petersburg, Yekaterinburg, Nizhny Novgorod, Novosibirsk and Samara. Journeys are cheap and fast, so up to nine million people travel the Moscow metro every day – more than the London and New York systems combined. Moscow's metro also vaunts lavish architecture, decorated with chandeliers, mosaics and statues.

Buses and trams are other important forms of public transport. St Petersburg has more trams than any other city in the world, and they carry about 950 million passengers a year.

Moscow's Krasnopresnenskaya metro station boasts spectacular architecture.

A Russian tourist stands admiring the ancient Acropolis in Athens, Greece.

During the communist era, few foreigners were allowed to enter the USSR, and there were heavy restrictions that made it difficult for its own citizens to travel abroad. During that time, most Russians holidayed within the USSR, and locations such as the Crimean coast (in Ukraine) were popular. Today, tourism is a rapidly developing industry in Russia, with foreign tourists contributing an estimated US$4 billion to the economy in 2002.

RUSSIAN TOURISTS

There are over 10,000 travel agencies in Russia, catering for the needs of Russian tourists, but only a quarter of them deal with domestic tourism (holidays within Russia). Sochi, on the Black Sea coast, is one of the most popular tourist destinations within Russia. Sochi's spa hotels (called *santorii*), which offer therapies to treat various ailments, are a popular attraction. The international film festival that is held there each June also draws many visitors.

Most travel agencies focus on international tourism. In 2000, 4.5 million Russians travelled abroad for holidays. If other journeys such as business trips are included, this figure increases to 18 million. Spain, Turkey and Cyprus are the most popular holiday destination for Russians.

VISITORS FROM ABROAD

In 2000, 6.8 million visitors visited Russia. Two million of these were business travellers, and only one third travelled from countries that are not part of the former USSR. Moscow and St Petersburg are high-profile tourist destinations. Russia's nature reserves, such as Baikal in Siberia, the Altai Mountains, the North Caucasus region and the Kamchatka Peninsula, are also gaining wider appeal among foreign tourists.

Some tourists experience frustration in Russia, owing to the problems of the language

INTERNATIONAL TOURIST ARRIVALS (THOUSANDS)

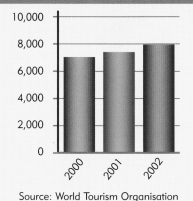

Year	Arrivals
2000	~7,000
2001	~7,400
2002	~8,000

Source: World Tourism Organisation

barrier, which can make everyday tasks like travelling on the metro a significant challenge. Other tourists are surprised by the relatively high cost of things like train and theatre tickets. There is a dual pricing system in Russia, which means that tourists have to pay higher prices than Russian citizens.

The government has launched a large campaign to make Russia a more popular tourist destination. Efforts have included restoration of historical buildings, new hotels and restaurants and improved facilities for disabled tourists. A new Formula One Grand Prix racetrack in southern Moscow (built at a cost of US$100 million) will hopefully be a magnet for Formula One enthusiasts.

TOURISM RECEIPTS (US$ MILLION)

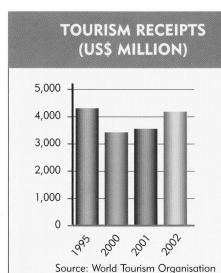

Year	Receipts
1995	~4,300
2000	~3,400
2001	~3,500
2002	~4,200

Source: World Tourism Organisation

CASE STUDY
SPACE TRAVEL FOR TOURISTS

Russia is pioneering space travel for tourists. In April 2001, Dennis Tito, an American billionaire, appeared on television screens all around the world, as he became the first paying customer of the Russian Space Agency. Tito paid US$20 million to make the week-long journey to the International Space Station, and spent several months training at Star City, not far from Moscow. The trip went without a hitch and, in April 2002, Mark Shuttleworth, a millionaire from South Africa, also made the journey.

Other Russian companies are putting together less expensive space travel programmes. For example, the Sub-Orbital Corporation will take tourists out of the atmosphere to experience weightlessness. This costs US$100,000, and up to 250 people have already paid a deposit to make the journey. Other cheaper options are also gradually appearing, making space travel more accessible.

US space tourist Dennis Tito gestures triumphantly after his space journey.

Students engaged in a Modern Languages lecture at St Petersburg University.

EDUCATION AND HEALTH

Free access to education and healthcare were important rights for all citizens of the USSR. However, funding was insufficient to ensure that schools, hospitals and communal housing were properly maintained. This lack of investment continues to affect life in Russia today.

EDUCATION

School is compulsory from the age of 7, and pupils must remain at school until they are 15, although most stay until they are 17. The literacy rate is close to 100 per cent, and most Russians are highly trained. State education is free, but the number of private schools is growing.

Russia inherited a system from the USSR in which schools were crowded, poorly maintained and teachers were badly paid. In the late 1980s, one fifth of all students studied in schools that had no central heating, and one third of pupils did not have access to running water during the school day. Teachers have always been respected in Russian society, but teaching was one of the lowest-paid professions in the early 1990s.

Since the collapse of communism, teachers have greater freedom from the state. Prior to 1991, teachers were expected to teach a standardised curriculum, which pupils were called upon to memorise. Nowadays, the curriculum is much broader, with greater emphasis on the humanities, arts and social sciences, although religious education is not taught in schools, despite pressure from the Church.

Teachers' pay has not improved much and schools are still in a state of disrepair, prompting some teachers to quit, frustrated by the continued lack of resources.

HEALTH

Health standards and life expectancy are falling across Russia. This is caused by several factors, including air and water pollution, overcrowded housing, poor nutrition, alcoholism and smoking. A lack of modern medical equipment

CASE STUDY
AIDS IN RUSSIA

Russia has one of the fastest growing HIV epidemics in the world. However, only about 4 per cent of people receive the treatment and medication that they need to prevent full-blown AIDS from developing. This means that the number of AIDS related deaths could rise sharply.

In a survey of people in Moscow, 70 per cent of people said that they felt fear, anger or disgust towards people who have the virus. Some people even believe that those with HIV should live in isolation.

To combat this prejudice and fear, a campaign to encourage tolerance towards HIV and AIDS was launched in May 2004. One television campaign stated: 'People among us are living with HIV ... but we can still talk to them and work together: we can still be friends.'

Russian students hold flags and posters at a rally for World AIDS Day 2004 in Moscow.

and inadequate training for doctors, nurses and paramedics also play a role.

Children are particularly at risk from poor health. Official statistics indicate that just one child in every five is born healthy. The problem is worsened by the fact that over half of Russian women are unable to breast-feed because of their own poor diet. Few children are immunised and, as a result, childhood diseases are common.

Contraception is not widely available across Russia and abortions, often carried out at a later stage when the procedure is more dangerous, are the most common form of contraception. Healthcare for other groups in society is also inadequate. Facilities for the six million disabled people living in Russia fall well below Western standards. Wheelchairs, ramps and artificial limbs are in extremely short supply.

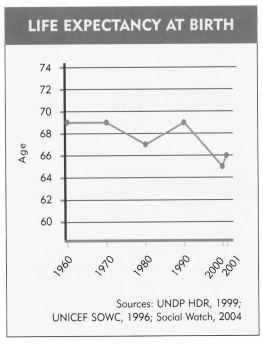

LIFE EXPECTANCY AT BIRTH

Sources: UNDP HDR, 1999;
UNICEF SOWC, 1996; Social Watch, 2004

CULTURE: RELIGION, ART, MUSIC AND LITERATURE

Russian Orthodox believers worship during a Christmas Eve service at the Church of the Icon of Our Lady of Kazan in Moscow.

For many years, the communist government suppressed religion and free cultural and artistic expression. The government of the USSR commissioned musical compositions and works of art, but they had to conform to the official political outlook. Today, with political restrictions lifted, Russian culture is being celebrated very publicly.

RELIGION

Out of all Russia's citizens who claim to be religious, 75 per cent are Russian Orthodox Christians. Many of them were fearful of expressing their belief openly during communist times, because the government was officially atheist (did not believe in the existence of God). Places of worship were infiltrated by the secret police on the look-out for people who did not uphold the views of the government. Bibles could only be bought on the black market.

However, churches across Russia are open once again. The number of men becoming priests has risen, and more children are being baptised. Even CDs of Russian monks chanting are available in shops.

Islam is the second largest religion in Russia with strongholds in regions like Chechnya. There are also Buddhist, Jewish and Shaman communities.

LITERATURE

Russian literature has a rich tradition, despite periods of strict censorship, when writers' work was closely monitored. When Gorbachev ended censorship, he sparked a reading frenzy across the USSR. Though, ironically, Russians now read less than they did before, leaving many current Russian writers with a sense of frustration.

Russian writers have created works that are acclaimed wordwide. For example, Dostoyevsky's *Crime and Punishment* and Tolstoy's novel *War and Peace*, are literary classics. Anton Chekhov's plays *The Cherry Orchard* and *The Seagull* are still performed across the world.

MUSIC

Russian musicians, composers and conductors are world-renowned. The Moscow Conservatoire has produced some of the brightest stars of the music world, including Sergei Rachmaninov, who produced many works for the piano and Peter Ilich Tchaikovsky, famous for his ballet music.

ART

Today, Russian artists are blazing a trail of experimentation. For example, Sergei Shutove represented Russia at the 2001 Venice Biennale, an international art exhibition. His exhibit consisted of 40 robots dressed in black, kneeling and reciting prayers.

CASE STUDY
ICONS

A Russian Orthodox patriarch prays in front of the Mother of God of Vladimir icon.

Icons are religious images painted on flat pieces of wood, using a type of paint made with egg yolk, and they are treated with great reverance (respect) by religious people. Many icons were painted by Greek artists invited to Russia, or their Russian pupils. They followed a style and tradition set by the Christian Byzantine Empire based in Constantinople (known today as Istanbul, the capital of Turkey).

One icon in particular, The Mother of God of Vladimir, is believed to be a prolific miracle worker. The icon is claimed to be one of three likenesses of the Virgin Mary painted by St Luke.

Legend states that the icon arrived in Kiev in the 1130s. Later, in 1155, Prince Andrei Bogolyubsky took the icon on a military campaign. As he crossed the River Klyazma the horses carrying it were unable to go on. Believing this to be a sign from God, the prince decided to build a church there.

The icon has been prominent throughout Russian history. It was taken into war, where soldiers believed that it sent out fiery rays to protect them. It was used during the coronation of Russia's tsars, and is said to have protected Moscow from invaders. The icon is now housed in the Tretyakov Gallery in Moscow.

FOOD AND DRINK

Eating and drinking are an important part of Russian life. Western influences are taking their toll, as McDonalds hamburger restaurants become more numerous, and Parisian-style cafés spring up in the streets of St Petersburg and Moscow. Nevertheless, regional specialities are still very important.

FOOD

Owing to the predominantly cold climate, energy-rich ingredients, such as potatoes, bread, eggs, meat and butter, are the main components of Russian food. Specialities include a range of soups such as *schi* (beef and cabbage) and the vibrantly purple *borscht* (made from pork and beetroot). Potatoes are usually fried, mashed or boiled.

Forest fruits and berries are used to make preserves, jams and puddings. *Bliny*, a type of pancake, are eaten with sweet foods such as honey, or with caviar as part of a savoury dish.

DRINK

The average Russian drinks 12 litres of pure alcohol each year, equating to a bottle of vodka a week. Men drink far more than women, and alcohol abuse is a grave problem causing many social and health problems.

Vodka is the most famous traditional beverage, and is usually made from rye or wheat. It is sometimes flavoured with pepper, berries or lemon. *Sbiten*, a drink made from honey, spices, water and vodka is another popular tipple. Beer is brewed in breweries across the country, and is extremely cheap. Tea is the non-alcoholic national drink, and is usually drunk in glasses without milk.

Street artists sip vodka to guard against temperatures of –20°C in the Russian capital.

Mayor of Moscow Yuri Luzhkov and Ukrainian President Leonid Kuchma in a Russkoye Bistro.

The fast-food industry is huge in Russia; it is worth US$650 million, a figure set to grow by 20 per cent each year. Unlike some other countries, where its popularity is declining, McDonalds draws many customers in Russia, with an 83 per cent share of the whole fast-food market. People are attracted to the promise of low-cost food and speedy service.

In order to challenge the power of McDonalds, Moscow's local government sponsored a chain of Russian cafés called Russkoye Bistro. They serve local fast food, such as sweet and savoury pies with tea and alcoholic drinks. The restaurants have had some success, but have hit some problems. By selling alcohol, customers are encouraged to linger, so fewer customers can be served each day. The quality of the food has also declined, as outlets have started to buy frozen semi-finished products, instead of making their own fresh, tastier pies.

Despite these difficulties, the Russkoye Bistro chain has expanded abroad, with a restaurant in Boston, USA.

HOSPITALITY

Russians are extremely hospitable. Guests who are invited to a Russian home for a meal will find tables groaning under the weight of numerous dishes. Alcoholic drinks and toasts (to say thank you) occupy a central part of every meal, and refusal to drink can cause deep offence. If tourists end up sharing a table in a bar or restaurant with local people, they will usually be invited to join them for drinks. Again, it is very difficult to decline.

KARAVAI

Karavai are special loaves of bread that look like cakes. They are baked especially for guests or newly-weds, and are presented to them as they enter the house.

Children ice-skating on a rink in Moscow's Red Square. Ice-skating is a popular pastime.

SPORT AND RECREATION

The athletes of the USSR were amongst the best in the world. Today, Russia continues to build on this sporting tradition, with victory for Maria Sharapova in the 2004 tennis final at Wimbledon, and medals from the 2004 Olympic games in disciplines ranging from athletics to rowing.

BANYAS

A *banya* is a Russian version of a sauna. Usually, a town has at least one *banya*, and it is a very popular, sociable place. People cover their skin in honey, then go into a hot steam room and beat themselves with birch twigs to stimulate the circulation. This is followed by a dip in an icy pool, although those who live in the countryside might roll in the snow instead.

Cooling off after a sauna (*banya*).

SPORT

Russia has an ideal climate for outdoor ice-skating, a popular hobby for many Russians. In winter, frozen ponds and artificial rinks fill with eager crowds. Ice-skating is a high profile sport after many winter Olympic successes over the years.

Organised sports clubs play a key role in Russian communities. There are many sports halls, swimming pools, football pitches and athletics tracks.

Russia's incredible mountain scenery has always attracted climbers, hikers and backpackers. During the communist days, the Soviet Mountaineering Federation made the mountain wilderness accessible to children from all over the country. Climbing and hiking clubs were well funded, and flourished as membership blossomed. Tragically, this funding has been cut. The mountain rescue service is chronically short of money, and so mountain trips are now more dangerous. Mountain trips have become too expensive for the majority of people.

OTHER LEISURE ACTIVITIES

Chess has a high profile in Russia. The country has produced several world champions, including Boris Spassky and Anatoly Karpov. On warm summer days, chess matches are often played in parks or on street corners.

Nightclubs and bars are very popular, with dance parties sometimes held on the islands in the Gulf of Finland. Television (particularly soap operas) also attracts many loyal viewers.

In the summer, many city-dwelling Russians seek tranquillity in the countryside. They retreat to their country houses (*dachas*) – small, unheated wooden cottages with gardens. Weekly steam baths (*banya*) are another important ritual for some.

The Russian ballet is world famous. The Bolshoi and the Kirov ballet companies are the most well known. Tickets can be expensive, but the dancers draw large audiences. Moscow also has two separate circuses that put on glitzy spectacles, including acrobats, animals, dance and cabaret.

Maria Sharapova, Wimbledon Champion in 2004 and finalist in the Australian Open in 2005, is the latest Russian tennis star. Maria was born in 1987 in Nyagan, a Siberian town, but later moved to Sochi, on the Black Sea coast. Encouraged by her parents, Maria started playing tennis at four years old, and was noticed by the Russian Tennis Federation in Moscow a couple of years later.

As Russia underwent a period of political upheaval during the early 1990s, Maria's parents were advised by Martina Navratilova, one of the greatest tennis players of all time, to take their daughter to the USA to further her tennis career. The move involved considerable sacrifice, as Maria's mother was unable to obtain a visa, and had to stay behind. Maria attended the famous Bollettieri Sports Academy, where she pursued an intensive training programme. Maria's athletic ability and star appeal have made her an undisputed international media figure.

Maria Sharapova clenches her arms in victory on winning the Wimbledon final, 2004.

CRIME

A major crime wave swept through Russia in the 1990s, and crime remains high today. Russia's murder rate is four times greater than that of the USA. In 2001, 33,500 people were murdered – most of them contract killings, carried out for as little as US$1,000. In total, over three million crimes were reported in 2001, ranging from burglary to corruption, drug smuggling and car theft. President Putin has vowed to take a hard line on crime, but his action is yet to make a significant impact.

An officer of a special Russian drugs task force arrests a drug dealer in the Kalauga region.

ORGANISED CRIME

The level of crime in Russia has been growing since the 1960s, when President Brezhnev was in power. Luxury goods were scarce and shops were empty, so professional criminals stepped in to provide them. The KGB (secret police) kept the level of crime under relative control.

When communism came to an end in the 1990s, organised crime escalated. Moscow-based mafia gangs grew more powerful, controlling prostitution, gun and drug smuggling. Experts believe that by the late 1990s, gangsters controlled 80 per cent of Russia's banks and managed 40 per cent of businesses.

Forbes magazine is a famous US business publication. In April 2004, *Forbes Russia* was launched, edited by an American journalist, Paul Khlebnikov.

A Moscow gunman murdered Khlebnikov in July 2004. Police believe that he may have been murdered because of his work – he had investigated Russian billionaire businessman Boris Berezovsky. He suggested that Berezovsky had ties with the Chechen mafia, and had smuggled millions of dollars out of Russia.

Khlebnikov is not the only journalist to have been murdered. In 2004 alone, five journalists were killed. These events demonstrate the problems of trying to establish a true democracy in Russia, where freedom of speech should be a top priority.

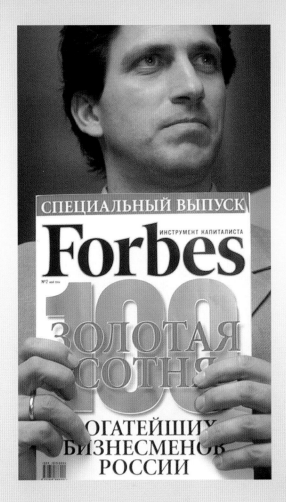

Paul Khlebnikov of *Forbes Russia* magazine in May 2004. He was killed two months later.

Corruption within the police force has made crime even harder to tackle. In St Petersburg, nicknamed the 'capital of crime', city police officers have been known to stop foreign tourists in the street at night, demanding to see their travel and identity documents and issuing unofficial fines.

DRUGS

Drug abuse and smuggling is also becoming more acute in Russia. There are between three and four million drug users in Russia, from all parts of society, and consumption was 23 times higher in 2002 than it was in 1998.

Drugs, especially heroin, have been highlighted in the media as a particular problem. About 70 per cent of heroin in Russia comes from Afghanistan. Crops of opium poppies – the plant used to make heroin – have boomed since the US-led war in Afghanistan in 2002, as impoverished farmers desperately try to make a living. Russia has set up a drug control committee to try and deal with the problem. Several drugs rings have been broken up, and in early 2004, Russian border guards confiscated 3.2 tonnes of drugs – mostly heroin.

COUNTERFEIT GOODS

Fake goods are a widespread problem. The Russian government has estimated that up to 90 per cent of all goods sold to consumers are not genuine. Electrical goods are mostly imported illegally from South-east Asia, and toys from China, but food, clothes, medicine and videos tend to originate from within Russia.

Fake drugs and alcohol put people at most risk. Every year, thousands of Russians die after drinking deadly chemicals that are sold as bottles of vodka.

The 4,750m high Kluchevskaya Sopka volcano on the Kamchatka Peninsula.

Natural hazards are natural events that take place in the physical environment that damage property and endanger human life. They are monitored carefully to minimise the damage they cause.

NATURAL HAZARDS

RECENT VOLCANIC ACTIVITY

The Kamchatkan Volcanic Eruption Response Team monitors active volcanoes on the Kamchatka Peninsula closely. Warnings and advice are posted on the Internet, and emergency procedures are carefully planned. A major eruption has not occurred for several years, but some volcanoes, such as Karymsky, regularly release clouds of ash up to 8,000m into the atmosphere.

EARTHQUAKES AND TSUNAMI

The Kuril Islands are prone to earthquakes and tsunami (giant, destructive waves generated by undersea earthquakes). The Earth's crust is made up of several tectonic plates that can move quite suddenly. Two of these plates, the Pacific plate and the North American plate meet beneath the Kuril Islands. The Pacific plate is being slowly sucked beneath the

North American plate and, as a result of this movement, there can be severe earthquakes.

At 00.23 am on 5 October 1994, there was a strong earthquake on the islands. It measured 8.1 on the Richter scale (a scale between 1 and 10 used to measure the intensity of earthquakes, where 10 is the most severe). Large cracks up to 350m long and 60m wide opened up in the ground and landslides stripped hillsides. The earthquake killed 11 people and injured 242. It also triggered a tsunami which claimed a further eight victims. The death toll would have been greater if the earthquake had occurred during the day, and if more people lived in the area.

DROUGHT

Droughts are caused by periods of hot, dry weather lasting one to three years. Russia was affected by a drought in 1998–99 that had a damaging effect on the grain harvest.

Parts of Siberia are prone to an unusual type of flooding in the spring. Many of Siberia's rivers, such as the River Ob, flow from the south to the north. They flood regularly when spring meltwater flowing from the warmer south backs up behind the frozen ice in the cooler north.

The River Ob flows north into the Kara Sea, where it divides into a series of finely braided streams (small channels separated by mud and silt). In June 2002, this area transformed itself into a 52km-wide lake as water spilled out of the river channel. The flooding affected towns and villages for hundreds of miles along the river.

Rescue workers search a bus swept into the Black Sea at Shirokaya Balka in 2002.

In the same year, floods hit the Black Sea coast, killing 55 people. Most casualties were local residents who drowned.

Permafrost Drought

Flooding Volcanic activity

NATURAL HAZARDS

Several areas where arable farming is important, such as the Volga region, suffered intense heat, with temperatures reaching 37°C – a point at which it is extremely difficult to water plants effectively. This period of drought followed a harsh, cold spring, where some plants had already been damaged by frost. The harvest was affected so severely that the government had to make an appeal to the international community for food aid.

ECOLOGICAL ISSUES

Human impact

Air pollution

Forest damage

River pollution and water shortage

Soil contamination and erosion

ENVIRONMENT AND WILDLIFE

Russia faces numerous environmental challenges, caused by a range of historical, economic and political factors. The future of Russia hangs in the balance until they can be addressed. The present situation, where catastrophic industrial pollution has led to the contamination of 50 per cent of Russia's water supplies, and the survival of unique habitats such as Lake Baikal is uncertain, cannot be sustained any longer.

However, Russia does not have the resources to combat these problems alone. Initiatives such as the Cross-Border Co-operation and Environmental Safety in Northern Europe Act of 2000, in which Russia has agreed to work with countries like Norway to reduce air pollution, are a step in the right direction. It is vital that there is a commitment from the government to continue this work, but this is difficult. President Putin has shown his commitment to Russia's economic growth, but he is yet to demonstrate his wholehearted support for the environment.

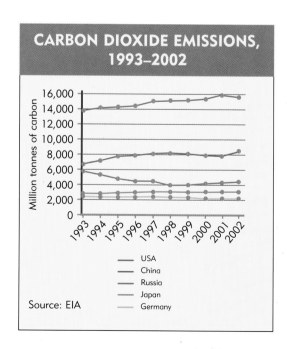

CARBON DIOXIDE EMISSIONS, 1993–2002

Million tonnes of carbon

16,000
14,000
12,000
10,000
8,000
6,000
4,000
2,000
0

1993 1994 1995 1996 1997 1998 1999 2000 2001 2002

USA
China
Russia
Japan
Germany

Source: EIA

At over 25 million years old, Lake Baikal (the 'Sacred Sea') is the world's oldest lake. It is shaped like a giant blue banana, stretching across south-east Siberia.

The lake is 636km long, 80km wide, and has 2,100km of coastline – equivalent to more than twice the length of the UK. It was formed when two plates of the Earth's crust collided, leaving a rift (deep gap) 9km deep. Over the last 25 million years, 7km of mud has accumulated at the lake bottom. Baikal is the world's deepest lake, reaching 1,637m on the western shore and holds 20 per cent of the world's liquid fresh water (more than all the water in the Great Lakes of the USA combined). Over 300 rivers and streams feed the lake. Thanks to the filtering action of millions of tiny crustaceans called *epishura*, the water is exceptionally clear; you can gaze down as far as 40 metres.

During the winter, when temperatures plummet as low as –35°C, the whole surface of the lake freezes over. Thermal springs at the bottom release oxygen into the water, keeping everything alive.

Weather on Baikal is governed by the lake's own micro-climate. Winds, known as *barguzin*, screech down from the river valleys at hurricane force, generating waves up to six metres high. People on the shore might never know, as storms usually die down before reaching the shoreline.

The lake is home to over 1,000 species (different types) of plants and animals that are not found anywhere else in the world. Perhaps the most famous resident of Baikal is the Baikal seal, or nerpa. It is the only freshwater seal in the world. The nerpa relies on *golomyanka*, a transparent, pink, oily fish for most of its food. Seal numbers have declined recently owing to pollutants in the food they eat, although the seal population still stands at approximately 50,000.

Water pollution is a real problem. Recent laws have tried to prevent nearby industries from dumping waste into the lake, but considerable damage has already been done.

There is hope of protecting Baikal. There are a number of protected areas, and a Baikal Commission was created in 1993 to administer and coordinate the federal and regional government efforts, as well as scientific experts and NGOs (non-governmental organisations) such as Baikal Watch, who have campaigned for the lake to become a world heritage site.

Nerpa seals bask on Lake Baikal. They are the lake's sole mammal species.

Autocracy A state governed by a single ruler.

Bolshevik Someone connected with the political system introduced by Lenin in 1917 in Russia, or a supporter of that system.

Capitalism An economic system in which the means of production (for example factories), distribution and sale are privately owned and operated for private profit.

Cold War A period during which there was political tension between Eastern and Western nations, particularly between the USSR and the USA.

Collective farm A farming unit made up of smaller farms that were joined together. They were closely supervised by the state.

Communism A group of political ideas based on the work of Karl Marx (1818–83). The main focus of communism is that the means of production are owned and controlled by all the members of society.

Deforestation Cutting down trees without replanting them.

Delta A landform, usually triangular in shape, created by a river when it deposits sand and silt upon entering a sea or lake.

Democracy Government by the people through elected representatives.

Depopulation A reduction in the number of people who live in a place.

Desertification The transformation of land into desert.

Ecosystem The contents of a particular environment, including all the animals and plants that live within it.

Erosion The wearing away of land by water, ice or wind.

GDP (Gross Domestic Product) The monetary value of goods and services produced by a country in a single year.

Glasnost A policy introduced by Gorbachev in the late 1980s. It literally means 'openness' and was designed to make the USSR government more open about the country's problems.

Global warming The increased global temperature caused by human activities that exaggerate the greenhouse effect. Certain gases within the atmosphere, such as carbon dioxide, absorb heat, keeping the Earth warm. Human activities such as the burning of fossil fuels increase the amount of greenhouse gases that are in the atmosphere, leading to higher global temperatures.

GNI (Gross National Income) The monetary value of goods and services produced by a country plus any earnings from overseas in a single year. It used to be known as Gross National Product (GNP).

Habitat The place or region where a plant or animal is naturally found.

HEP (Hydroelectric power) Electricity that is produced using water power.

Industrialisation The process where industry becomes the primary activity of a society.

Inflation A general rise in prices. Inflation arises when there is more currency and credit available relative to the number of goods available to buy.

Migration The movement of people from one place to another.

Oligarch Derived from a Greek word meaning 'rule by the few'. The Russian oligarchs are an elite group of people who control most of Russia's large companies, banks and industries. They are extremely wealthy.

Peninsula A piece of land that is almost an island, either connected to the mainland by a narrow neck or projecting into the sea, with the sea on three sides.

Perestroika An economic policy introduced by Gorbachev in the late 1980s, to restructure the economy. The aim of *perestroika* was to boost economic growth.

Permafrost Lower layers of soil (subsoil) that are permanently frozen.

Revolution The unconstitutional overthrow of a country's established government or leader.

Russian Soviet Federal Socialist Republic (RSFSR) The main republic of the former USSR.

Shaman A priest or witch doctor who uses magic to mediate with gods and spirits, foretell the future and heal.

Shamanism The religion practised by a Shaman.

Soil erosion The wearing away and transportation of the soil layer.

Soviet An elected governing council within the former USSR. Soviets were originally revolutionary committees elected by the factory workers after the revolution of 1905. The term was then used to describe the primary units of government within the USSR at local, provincial and national level.

Union of Soviet Socialist Republics (USSR) A federal republic founded in 1922. It consisted of 15 constituent republics, each inhabited by a major national group. Moscow was the capital of the USSR. The republics within the USSR were: The Russian Soviet Federal Socialist Republic (RSFSR), Ukraine, Kazakhstan, Uzbekistan, Belarus, Georgia, Azerbaijan, Moldavia, Lithuania, Kyrgyzstan, Tajikistan, Latvia, Armenia, Turkmenistan and Estonia.

FURTHER INFORMATION

BOOKS TO READ:

The Endless Steppe by Esther Hautzig (HarperCollins, 1989) A true story about a Jewish family from Poland, exiled to Siberia in 1941.

In Siberia by Colin Thubron (Penguin Books, 2000) A travel story describing a journey through Siberia and the people met along the way.

Lonely Planet Guide: Russia, Ukraine and Belarus by John Noble (Lonely Planet Publications, 2000) Budget travel guide for travellers of all ages. Good background information sections.

One Day in the Life of Ivan Denisovitch by Alexander Solzhenitsyn (Penguin Modern Classics) A short, readable novel describing a day in the life of a prisoner in a Siberian gulag (prison camp).

Stalingrad by Anthony Beevor (Penguin Books, 1999) A detailed explanation of the battle for Stalingrad in the Second World War, interspersed with personal accounts.

FOR OLDER READERS:
Russia In The Modern World: A New Geography by Denis J.B. Shaw (Blackwell Publishers, 1999)

WEBSITES:

The US Energy Information Administration
http://www.eia.doe.gov/emeu/cabs/russenv.html
This site summarises Russia's environmental issues.

The Mandela Projects
http://www.american.edu/TED/class/all.htm
An excellent site with very detailed articles and case studies.

The US Geological Survey
http://volcanoes.usgs.gov/update.html#russia
This page provides regular updates about the activity of Russian volcanoes.

Caviar Emptor
http://www.caviaremptor.org
For further information on the decline of the sturgeon fish.

Anne Applebaum
http://www.anneapplebaum.com/gulag/intro.html
A helpful site giving a history of the gulags.

The CIA World Factbook
www.cia.gov/cia/publications/factbook/geos/rs.html
The US Central Intelligence Agency's online factbook, with statistics and assessments of all countries in the world.

FILM:

Nicholas and Alexandra Directed by Franklin J. Schaffner (1971) This film describes the events of the Russian Revolution in 1917, and the fall of the last Russian tsar, Nicholas II.

Goodbye Lenin Directed by Wolfgang Becker (2003) A German film set in 1989–90 when the Berlin Wall came down. The story tells of a family who try to re-create a communist world for their mother, as they are worried that the shock of finding that the Cold War has ended, might kill her.

Doctor Zhivago Directed by David Lean (1965) Oscar-winning film based on the novel by Boris Pasternak detailing the life of a Russian doctor and poet during the first half of the twentieth century.

Numbers shown in **bold** refer to pages with maps, graphic illustrations or photographs.

A monastic settlement on
Krestovy Island, Lake Ladoga.
The lake freezes in winter.